NOTES IN THE ATTIC

a

Notes

in the Attic

Scribbler

Domesday Books

Title: Notes in The Attic
Author: Scribbler
Publisher Domesday Books
ISBN 978-1-7325730-0-0
Copyright ©2018Domesdaybooks

All rights reserved. No part of this publication may be reproduced, distributed, or transmitted in any form or by any means, including photocopying, recording, or other electronic or mechanical methods, without the prior written permission of the publisher, except in the case of brief quotations embodied in critical reviews and certain other noncommercial uses permitted by copyright law.

Domesday Books
P.O.Box 8625 Norfolk VA 23503 USA

For Mother

Table of contents

Contents

Heaven 1

Aunt's Wedding Day 5

I Sing 6

(written for my musician friends) 6

Stay with Me 9

(written for musician friends) 9

Anika 12

Autumn 15

How 17

Seasons of Spring in Japan 19

Bicycle 21

A Little Heart Warmer 23

In her letter 25

St. Anthony's Turnip 27

Shampoo 29

To Joshua 31

Kitten 35

Granddad 37

Black Thumb 39

Gazing Up the Midnight Sky 42

Poem 43

A Lady Raking Leaves 45

Life 47

Granny 51

Crush 53

Adult Nappy 54

Rainy London 55

London 56

Son 59

Loneliness 61

Happiness 65

My Utmost Gratitude 66

About Scribbler 66

Heaven

Heaven

    Doubtless it's a marvelous place

    Everyone wants to go to heaven

Revelation revealed

There will be no tears or pain

God will be in heaven

He wants to be your friend

He wants to dwell with you

And wipe away all your tears

Heaven

    The perfect place

    Beautiful gardens

    Perfect unselfish love governs

    All relationships in heaven

Perfect place?

    How perfect?

Isaiah said

The former things will not be remembered

Nor will they come to mind

If heaven is such a perfect place

    with no tears or pain

    what happens to compassion?

    How about empathy?

    We can't feel other's pain?

    We can't remember

    the struggle of the less fortunate?

I don't want to lose the ability

    to feel other people's pain and sadness

    their loneliness and sorrow

I want to remember

    kindness people showed me

    love people shared with me

We have a name for that here

It's called life

Do I really want to go to heaven?

Aunt's Wedding Day

On her wedding morning

She sits properly on the floor

    clad in pearly white silk wedding kimono

Her parents sit on the floor too

    facing their daughter

She slowly bows to them

    putting her hands on the floor

She offers the greeting tumultuously

    Father, Mother

    Thank you very much for

    everything you have done to raise me

Parents proudly nod fighting back tears

She's beautiful in the bridal white

    It's also a funeral white

For this is also the day

    her innocence dies

I Sing

(written for my musician friends)

Said good bye to my love and

      left the land of my childhood

      with the guitar in my hand

      for the journey of my life

I played Rock and Roll in a band

      sang many songs of love

Life's been good to me

      the whole world turns around me

But what haunts me is my regret

Somewhere deep in my heart

      lives a girl I once loved

She is my song, my living ghost

      yearning for my living voice

So I sing

Never looking back the past

  Climbing up the ladder of human race

  to catch the world in my hand

  for the success of my life

I play Rock and Roll in a band

sing many songs of love

Life's been indulging

  the whole world turns around me

But what haunts me is my regret

Somewhere deep in my heart

  lives a girl I can't forget

She is my song, my living ghost

  yearning for my living voice

So I sing

  I sing

  I sing

Stay with Me
(written for musician friends)

Girl

You've been my refuge

      when my heart and soul are shattered

      and the hardship brings me to my knees

The night is near

      stay with me

      for the end is near

Keep my soul for me

      stay with me

      through the darkest silent hours

      Keep my soul for me

Girl

Your name was my prayer

      when my fear and tears called your name

and the silence pierce through my spine

The night is near

    stay with me

    for the end is near

Keep my soul for me

    stay with me

    through this thorny lonely night

Girl

You've been my Sanctuary

    where I could escape from times of trouble

The night is near

    stay with me

    for the end is near

Keep my hope for me

    stay with me

while I wait for dawn to break

Anika

Once upon a hope

Born was the treasure

Your fairest hair

Your killer smile

Giving people such a pleasure

And your bluest eyes dare

Ready to charm the world

Anika Wake up the world needs you

Anika Wake up you're sleeping too long

Anika Wake up we're all waiting for you

Anika Wake up mum is there beside you

One upon a hope

Your days got harder

Knocked you down the slippery slope

The toils and troubles much harsher

But you took courage

Ready to fight the woe

Once upon the pain

God pulled you aside

Kept you through the toughest time

Can you hear us, my dear Anika

Rise again to taste your victory

With your bluest eyes dare

Ready to charm the world

Wake up the world needs you

Wake up you're sleeping too long

Wake up we're all waiting for you

Wake up mum is there

Anika We love you

Autumn

Let's go for a walk

      and greet the new autumn

See the high sky

Feel the summer's afterglow

Look at the sunning colours of leaves

Leaves are scattered in the air

      and falling and falling and falling

Let's go for a walk

      and meet the new autumn

How

How was I born?

    A little boy asked his family

Because We wanted to love you

    Answered his granny

Seasons of Spring in Japan

The first the day of spring comes

It's the day spring starts on calendar

The first wind is *Haru Ichiban*

Water they get from a well

    on the First Day of Spring

    is called the Young Water

    which removed evil things for the year

Season of the east wind is the spring wind

    which begins melting thick ice

Season of bush warbler's voice

    the first sound of spring people waited for

Season of fish jumping out of ice

    when they sense spring is come

Season of rain

    winter snow changes to spring rain

Season of the earth

   when it prepares for new life

   Hepatica is the most impatient of all

Season of mountains

   they will be dressed in fog

Season of germination

   when every rain brings new life

Bicycle

My son's bikes

    kept in the fenced backyard

    were stolen many times

    The thief covered them with new paint

    Took them apart for the parts

What was left would be ditched somewhere

You had to see your bikes were violated

I had to see you heart broken

    It ripped my heart too

The last time your bike was stolen

    It happened on a playground

    before our eyes

It happened too fast

    I couldn't stop it

    I couldn't protect you

    I'm sorry I let you down

A Little Heart Warmer

One day Little Stephen said to me

When I grow up

I will buy you bunny slippers

How sweet of you, Stephen

It made my feet warm already

In her letter

I found an old letter from Mother

It said when she was pregnant with me

    doctor found a problem with her womb

She was told to abort me for a surgery

Grandma said

    No you do not do such a thing

She took her pregnant daughter

    from doctor to doctor

They found a university hospital could help her

She had the surgery

    when she was four month pregnant

I was born

during a howling winter storm at 2:50 am

My mother was the only child

    hoped that I and my younger sister

    would give her many grandchildren

That one simple dream she secretly kept

        was shattered when I left the country

Her letter gave out a silent cry

        of a lonely mother

        who kept giving so much love

I folded the letter to shut her cry

        Something sharp stabbed my heart

St. Anthony's Turnip

It was like this every morning

      we would walk Josh to school

Sweet yellow bulbous buttercups

St. Anthony's Turnip they call it

Gently blooming everywhere

Hurry up hurry up Little Steven

      Josh will be late for school

Hold on hold on

      I'm coming

      I picked these for you

St. Anthony's Turnips

You were sweeter than the buttercups

How I wished you'd never grow up

Shampoo

Ambiguous dream spinning in my head

I can't grasp what it means

It spins inside my head

      stuck to my mind

      like old chewing gum

Trying to shake it off

      as I shampoo

To Joshua

We couldn't wait for the sun to rise

While the city was still asleep

    we walked 1.7 miles

    with you, at the 9th month in my womb

    on a dark and quiet 7th street

    anxious and scared

    fainthearted and afraid

    to the hospital on Elm street

    to give birth to you

    to welcome you to this world

    to be the first ones to love you

Oh, but the sequence of merciless pains

    there's no way to escape

From the days of Adam and Eve

    we were cursed with childbirth pain

God has kept his promises

lying on the delivery table

my lower abdomen tightened

hours of ruthless contractions

pounding pain

as this life tried to be born

Oh but the sequence of God's doubtless care

Between the contractions was the peaceful rest

    as he does throughout our lives

    however difficult your life might be

    in the mist of hardships

    God's blessing is never absent

After hours of excruciating pain

    you were born

    healthy and good natured

    loved so much by everyone

    who saw you

This is how you were born

        no accident nor mistake

        sought and wished for

        desired and wanted

I hope you will remember

I fought the pain to have you

Kitten

I wasn't going to look

I wasn't going to stop

Lost kitten by the brook

I'm not allowed to adopt

This abandoned kitten I held

Her warmth I felt

Granddad

We went to a hospital

    to visit granddad

He hasn't got long to go

His time fast nearing

He wants to thank everybody

Tried his best to leave messages

He put his hands together on his chest

    and closed his eyes

    with his rosy cheeks

Grandma flipped those hands

    told him to quit joking

Black Thumb

Some people have a green thumb

I seem to have a black thumb

I could kill a plastic flower

One day

A friend gave me a small pot of flowers

Put it by the kitchen window she said

    You can't kill it

But it died

I got a new pot

    put in some dirt and flower seeds

Soon a green plant started to come out

How exciting I thought

I kept watering every day

And it grew and grew

No sign of a flower yet

But the green got taller and taller

How encouraging I thought

Little did I know

        I'd been watering weed for two weeks

Gazing Up the Midnight Sky

Gazing up the late-night sky

    Glimmering stars silently shine

    The untold wishes secretly withheld

    quietly open in the still of the night

    Awe-striking

    overflowing magnificence

    And I felt mother's love

    as a shooting star beaconed

Gazing up the midnight sky

    Glistening stars silently shine

    The untold hopes dreamed and cherished

    Quietly awaken in the still of the night

    Awe-striking magnificence

    And I felt mother's love

    as a shooting star beaconed

Poem

Screw the rules

    It doesn't need to rhyme

Words are sacred jewels

Unlock them and watch them shine

    Watch them dance

    Hear them speak

    Feel their souls

    And they will be refined

A Lady Raking Leaves

There was a small shrine

    Manless and quiet among trees

When I was a child

    I walked there to pick some acorns

I was all alone and enjoying it

Suddenly out of nowhere

    I saw a lady

She was so infused with grace

    in a maroon kimono

    with her hair neatly up in a bun

    gently raking the colourful fallen leaves

Where did she come from?

With a smile of such elegance

    She answered

    I came from faraway

I thought I would go back to acorn picking

And I turned around

She was gone

There I stood mystified

    in front of the noman's shrine

    on the well-kept sacred ground

    surrounded by trees

    as yellow and orange leaves rained

Life

Life is like a tree

It has its roots grounded to the origin

You grow according to your kind

You grow branches and flowers

    according to your kind

You bear your yearly fruits

    according to your kind

You pray to God

    to take away your problem branches

You pray to God

    to give you what you need for growth

God hears your prayers

    He takes the troubles away

God hears your prayers

    He gives you what you need

Day after day, year after year

Still we let problems grow

bear bad fruits

for your roots are grounded

Until one day

God lifts you up whole

Granny

Every kid needs one of those

Every kid loves granny

She is sweeter than your mother

Superior than your father

Granny's kind of dry

Like an autumn leaf

Not at all sticky like your mother

Crush

There he is

      He's coming this way

Be brave and go

Tell him you that you like him

Hurry and go

You only have a moment

You'll miss the chance

Adult Nappy

TV adverts about paper undie

It fits you perfect

        They can't tell you are wearing it

Rather fashionable too

High quality and highly-absorbent

It absorbs your social status and dignity too

Rainy London

Steady rain soothes sound of busy traffic

Headlights floating on the streets

Everything is grey and chic

Umbrellas are migrating on the streets

Red double-deckers awkwardly crawl

      maneuvering in space so small

Pedestrians wordlessly hurry home

      where it's warm

I sit by a café's window

      watching dew on the window run

London

You've got the style

You've got the character

Essentially traditional

    with the weight of breeding

    and exclusiveness lurking behind

Always elegant based on wealth

    alluding to where you live, how you live

How you talk and what car you drive and more

It's all in the class

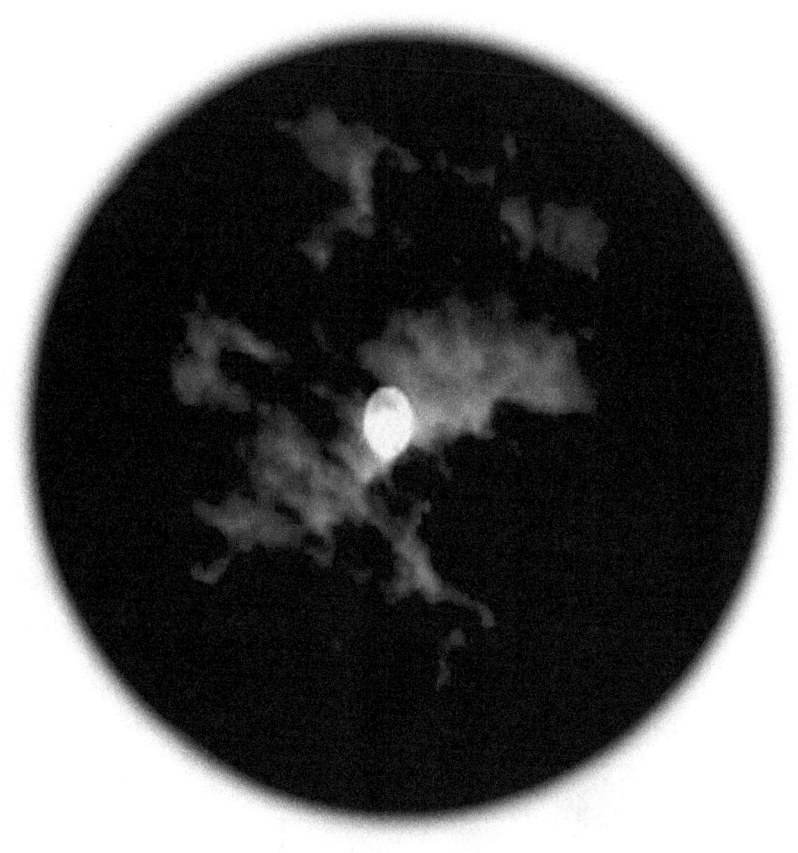

Son

Your day has been longer than mine

    But God has brought you safely home

Your task was harder than mine

    But God has brought you safely home

Deputy's job is tough and rough

    You were forced to toughen up

Every morning you wake up

    Facing the thought of death

Weekend army alone is tough enough

Put away the gun

    Now you are done

Take off the best

    It's time to rest

Lay down your anxious thoughts

    Forget your tought

Sweet Dreams

Loneliness

Maybe

That's what makes us capable of loving others

Maybe

That's what makes us

    capable of seeing the truth

And maybe

That's the best opportunity

    to enhance ourselves

Autumn

Sky has lifted its ceiling

Bluer is the autumn sky

Summer memory reeling

Clearer is the autumn sky

In such an idyllic season

Why do Leaves hurry to fall?

Leaves lay with their undoubting faith

On the lonely autumn mall

Covering the earth wait for their unknown fate

God's creatures and bacteria begin to crawl

To help each leaf back to the earth

To God each leaf is worth

Happiness

Happiness is

      to have someone in your heart

Sadness is

      to be rejected from your heart

Happiness is

      to give you love

Sadness is

      to share no love

Happiness is

      to be able to die thanking you

Sadness is

      to have to leave you with regret

My Utmost Gratitude To

God the Father

Vesna Velkovrh Bukilica and Tara Moeller for their wisdom, endless teaching, support, encouragement, kindness, guidance and friendship, which I am forever grateful.

Joshua and Stephen Smith
My Mother and the Morimoto Clan
My Father and Matsunaga Clan

About Scribbler

Freelance translator and scribbling writer.

Born in Fukuoka, Japan in 1964. Graduated from Fukuoka University with BA in Germanistik. London lover, Hesse lover, rock lover, coffee lover, comedy lover and a cat lover (but can't have any) Lives in Virginia USA.

www.ingramcontent.com/pod-product-compliance
Lightning Source LLC
Chambersburg PA
CBHW032212040426
42449CB00005B/558